the ultimate

VISION

BOARD

clip art book

VOL 2

2023
Reflection

WHAT WENT WELL IN 2023:

WHAT DIDN'T GO WELL IN 2023:

THINGS I NEED TO LET GO OF (FEARS, OPINIONS, EMOTIONS, DIETS, ETC.):

VISION Wheel

FOR EACH SECTION OF THE WHEEL, THINK ABOUT HOW HAPPY YOU ARE ON A SCALE OF 1 TO 10 AND THEN COLOR IT IN. USE DIFFERENT COLORS IF YOU LIKE!

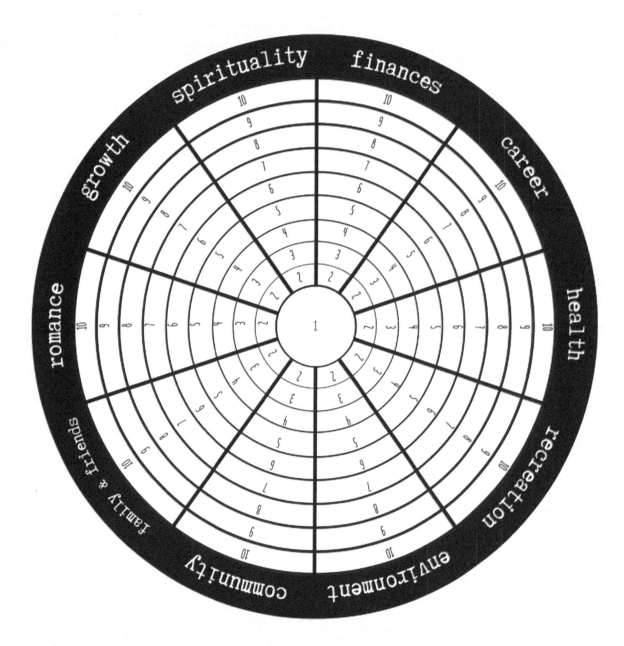

HOW BALANCED DOES YOUR WHEEL LOOK? IF IT LOOKS A LITTLE BUMPY, TAKE NOTICE BUT DON'T WORRY ABOUT IT. IT'S NORMAL TO HAVE AREAS IN YOUR LIFE THAT ARE HIGHER OR LOWER. TAKE NOTE, AND FOCUS ON THOSE AREAS THAT COULD DO WITH A LITTLE SHOVE IN THE RIGHT DIRECTION WHEN YOU MAKE YOUR VISION BOARD. THE SECTIONS WITH THE LOWER SCORES ARE USUALLY THE AREAS WE CARE ABOUT MOST.

ALL ABOUT *Me*

THINGS I'M GRATEFUL FOR:

THINGS I'M PASSIONATE ABOUT:

THINGS THAT MAKE ME HAPPY:

MY HOBBIES AND INTERESTS:

THREE WORDS THAT DESCRIBE ME:

THINGS THAT I'M GOOD AT:

....

....

....

....

A DIFFICULT CHALLENGE I'VE
OVERCOME:

....

....

....

MY IDEAL DAY LOOKS LIKE THIS:

....

....

....

FAVOURITE QUOTE:

....

....

....

....

IMPORTANT PEOPLE IN MY LIFE:

....

....

....

BAD HABITS I'D LIKE TO CHANGE:

....

....

....

NEW SKILLS I'D LIKE TO LEARN:

....

....

BOOKS I'D LIKE TO READ:

PLACES I WANT TO VISIT:

ADVENTURES I'D LIKE TO TRY

NEW MEALS TO TRY:

CHARITIES TO DONATE TO

RELATIONSHIPS TO WORK ON:

I'M GOING TO TREAT MYSELF TO:

ALL ABOUT
My Goals

CAREER GOALS:

_____
_____
_____
_____

FINANCIAL GOALS:

_____
_____
_____

FAMILY GOALS:

_____
_____
_____

RELATIONSHIP GOALS:

_____
_____
_____

TRAVEL GOALS:

_____
_____
_____

CAR GOALS:

_____
_____
_____

HOME GOALS:

_____
_____
_____

OTHER GOALS:

_____

NOTES

NOTES

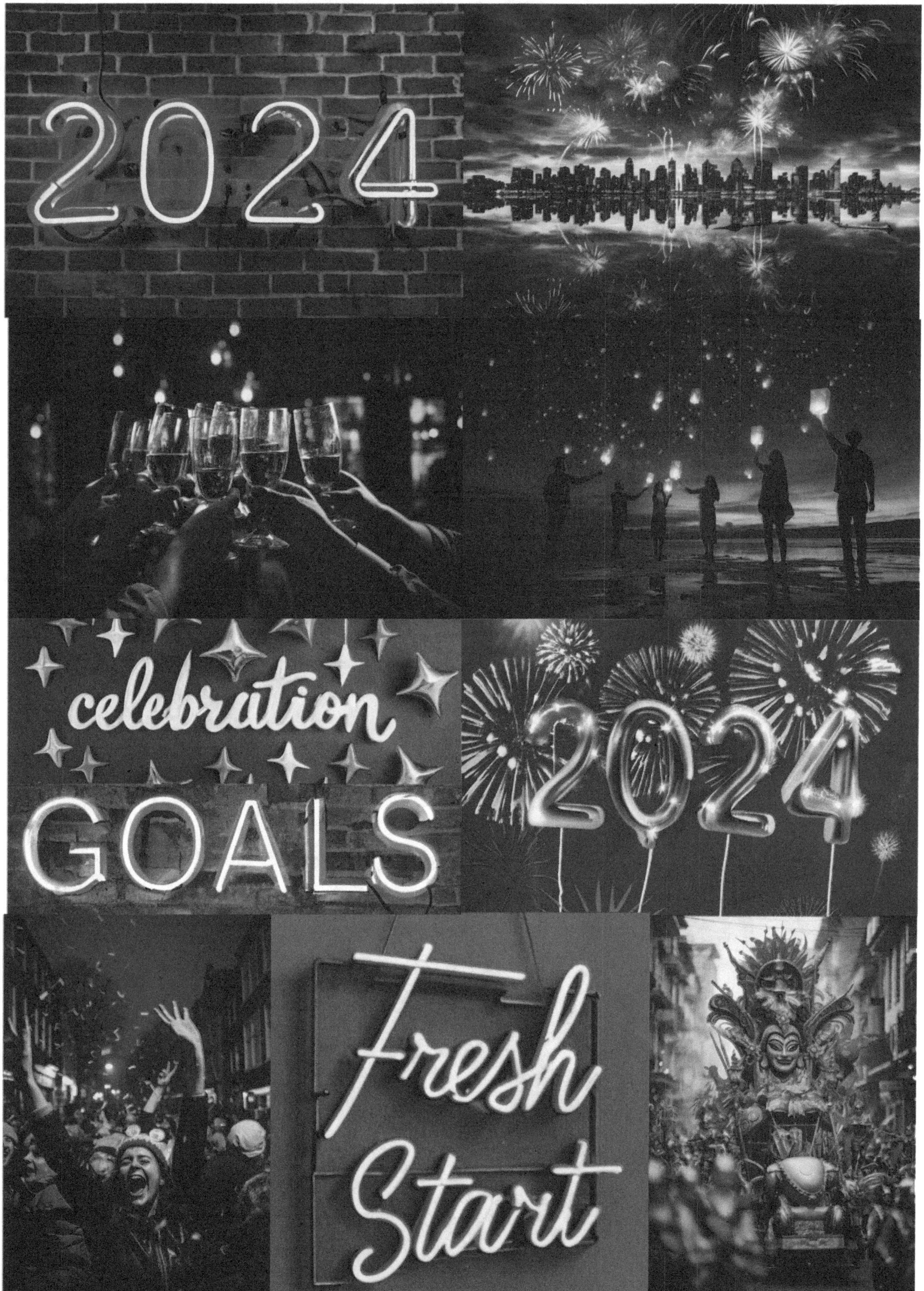
2024
celebration
GOALS
2024
Fresh
Start

SEE THE WORLD

TRAVEL

GOALS

DESTINATION UNKNOWN

DREAM

VACATION

ADVENTURE

BUCKET LIST

PACK

YOUR BAGS

GLOBETROTTER

JET SETTER

DISCOVER

BRAZIL MEXICO AUSTRALIA

MALDIVES SCOTLAND FRANCE

SOUTH AFRICA JAPAN BALI

NEW ZEALAND INDIA ITALY

THAILAND EUROPE ICELAND

MOSCOW CUBA CHINA SPAIN

BAHAMAS FINLAND IRELAND

MALDIVES BORA BORA PERU

MOROCCO GREECE NEW YORK

CROATIA ITALY MALAYSIA

VANCOUVER HAWAII DUBAI

LOS ANGELES COSTA RICA

UNIVERSAL AIRLINES

Boarding Pass

Boarding Pass

Passenger Name

Flight
AB 1234

Seat
15A

From

Date

Gate
A5

To

0 1 2 3 4 5 6 7 8 9

Boarding Time
10:00 AM

Passenger Name

From

To

Flight
AB 1234

Seat
15A

Gate
A5

Boarding Time
10:00 AM

UNIVERSAL AIRLINES

Boarding Pass

Boarding Pass

Passenger Name

Flight
AB 1234

Seat
15A

From

Date

Gate
A5

To

0 1 2 3 4 5 6 7 8 9

Boarding Time
10:00 AM

Passenger Name

From

To

Flight
AB 1234

Seat
15A

Gate
A5

Boarding Time
10:00 AM

UNIVERSAL AIRLINES

Boarding Pass

Boarding Pass

Passenger Name

Flight
AB 1234

Seat
15A

From

Date

Gate
A5

To

0 1 2 3 4 5 6 7 8 9

Boarding Time
10:00 AM

Passenger Name

From

To

Flight
AB 1234

Seat
15A

Gate
A5

Boarding Time
10:00 AM

UNIVERSAL AIRLINES

Boarding Pass

Boarding Pass

Passenger Name

Flight
AB 1234

Seat
15A

From

Date

Gate
A5

To

0 1 2 3 4 5 6 7 8 9

Boarding Time
10:00 AM

Passenger Name

From

To

Flight
AB 1234

Seat
15A

Gate
A5

Boarding Time
10:00 AM

I embrace my authenticity

INFLUENCER

FOLLOWERS

★★★★★

I create content that inspires, entertains & engages

ENGAGEMENT

BRANDING

ROLE MODEL

I get paid for being me

CONSISTENCY

100K
Followers

ONLINE STORE

DREAM JOB

I AM EARNING LOTS OF MONEY DOING WHAT I LOVE

I am confident and successful

CAREER

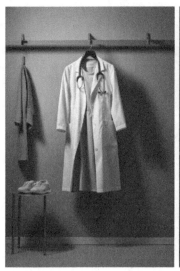

START YOUR
SIDE HUSTLE

like a boss

AMBITION

PAYRISE CEO

passive income

MILLIONAIRE

MINDSET

FINANCIAL
FREEDOM

money magnet

$$$ $ $ $

DEBT FREE

I DESERVE TO
LIVE A LIFE OF
LUXURY

I WAS BORN TO BE RICH

crypto currency

MONEY. LOTS OF IT.

FIRST CLASS

MILLIONAIRE

Wealth constantly flows into my life

PROPERTY

INVESTMENTS

STOCK
MARKET

I ♥ MONEY

i don't
chase money;
it chases me

*making
money is
my
superpower*

CELINE

GUCCI

**DOLCE &
GABBANA**

BALENCIAGA

I am
creating the
life of my
dreams

I ATTRACT
ABUNDANCE
AND WEALTH
INTO MY LIFE
EFFORTLESSLY

FREELANCE

E-COMMERCE

affiliate
marketing

RICH

THE PLAZA

LAUCALA ISLAND RESORT

MANDARIN ORIENTAL

THE RITZ PARIS

BANK OF THE UNIVERSE

$ Date: _____

Pay: _____

_____ $ _____

_____ Dollars

The Universe

AUTHORIZED SIGNATURE

0123456 789 87654321   0123456 789 87654321

BANK OF THE UNIVERSE

$ Date: _____

Pay: _____

_____ $ _____

_____ Dollars

The Universe

AUTHORIZED SIGNATURE

0123456 789 87654321   0123456 789 87654321

BANK OF THE UNIVERSE

$ Date: _____

Pay: _____

_____ $ _____

_____ Dollars

The Universe

AUTHORIZED SIGNATURE

0123456 789 87654321   0123456 789 87654321

I AM ATTRACTING A
PARTNER WHO LOVES ME
FOR WHO I AM

FIT SEXY STRONG

HANDSOME PASSIONATE KIND

loving honest

funny

I AM EXCITED TO CREATE
A BEAUTIFUL FUTURE
WITH THE PARTNER OF
MY DREAMS

RELATIONSHIP

SENSITIVE

INTELLIGENT

THOUGHTFUL

respectful

supportive

GENEROUS

empathetic

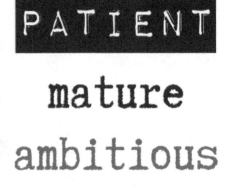

PATIENT

mature

ambitious

LOYAL

adventurous   artistic

CONFIDENT   athletic

my partner is my
best friend

SOULMATE

LOVE

TRUST

CONNECTION

DEVOTION

intimacy

my heart is open, and
i welcome love with
arms wide

i am worthy of love
and affection

I ATTRACT LOVING AND
CARING PEOPLE INTO MY LIFE

ROMANCE

passion

commitment

UNITY

YOU & ME

commitment

engaged!

WEDDING

Certificate of Marriage

This Certifies that

_____ and _____

were united in marriage on

_____

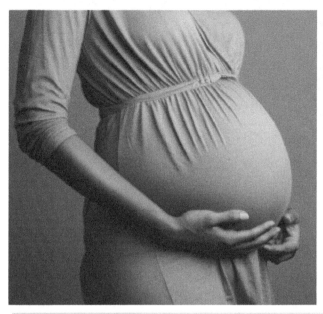

GENERAL HOSPITAL
Certificate of Birth

This Certifies *that*_____

weight _____ *lbs.* _____ *oz. was born in this Hospital*

on the _____ *day of* _____

In Witness Whereof this Certificate has been duly signed by the Happy Parents.

_____

PARENTS

it's a boy!

it's a girl!

motherland

new chapter

MY MIND AND BODY
ARE OPEN AND
READY TO RECEIVE A
NEW LIFE

I TRUST MY BODY AND
IT'S ABILITY TO CONCEIVE
A HEALTHY BABY

FAMILY

blessings

forgiveness

FAMILY: WHERE QUIRKS, CRAZINESS, AND UNCONDITIONAL LOVE COLLIDE

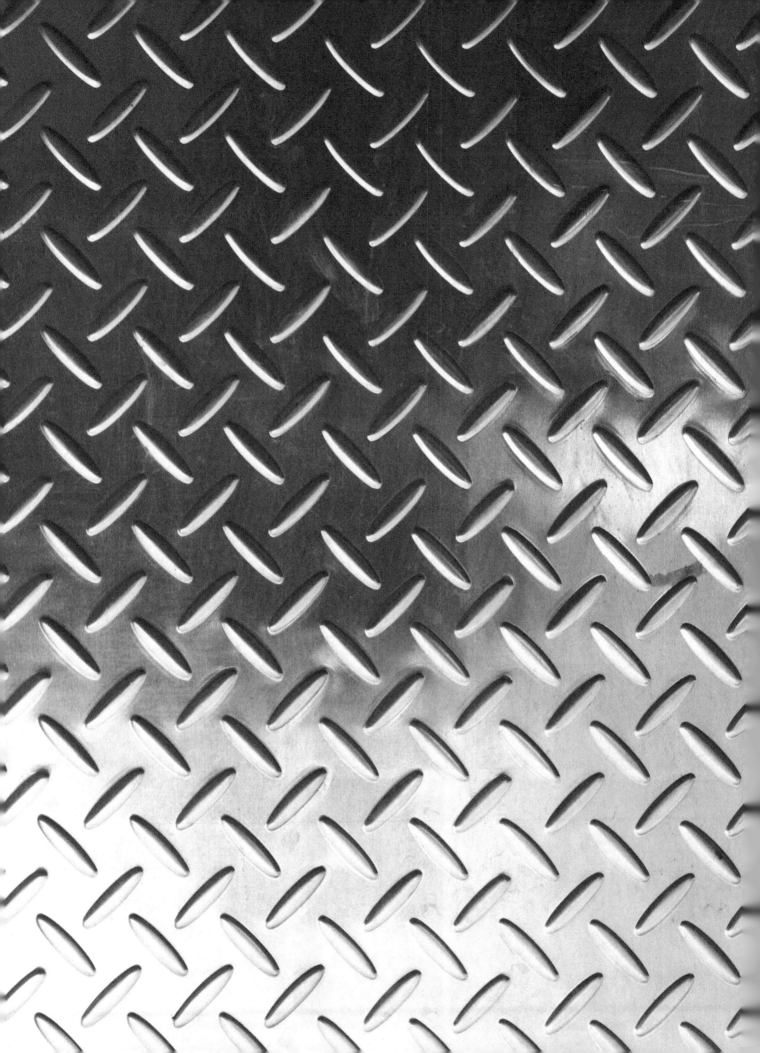

DRIVER LICENSE

Name

D.O.B

OFFICIAL

PORSCHE

LEXUS

MERCEDES

TESLA

AUDI BMW

RANGE HONDA

ROVER VOLVO

I am driving the car of my dreams!

electric
car

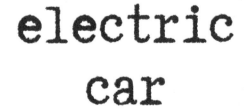

NEW CAR

LEARN TO DRIVE

GET MY LICENSE

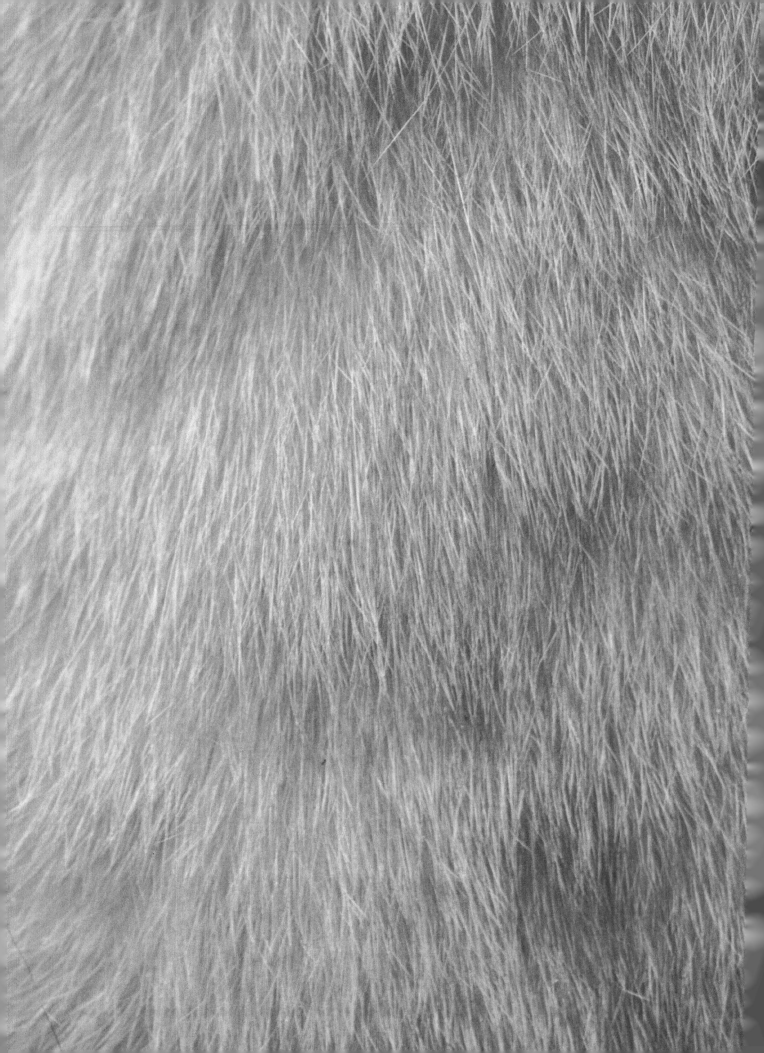

PONY

MEOW

DOG MOM

DOG

CAT

PET

my pet brings
joy and love
into my life

DREAM HOME

HOME OWNER

New Home

I'M EXCITED TO CREATE HAPPY MEMORIES IN MY NEW HOME

My home is filled
with lots of love.
And plants.

ROMANTIC

ORGANIC

boho vibes

relax NATURAL HARMONY

creative

CALM *Peaceful* RUSTIC

INNOVATIVE

loft style

INDUSTRIAL

URBAN

metropolitan

APARTMENT

CITY VIEW

architectural

MODERN

contemporary

CHIC

MINIMALIST

spacious

LIGHT

COSMOPOLITAN

mountain view

Farmhouse

COUNTRY LIFE

Warm & Cozy

warm by the fire

homely

grow my own food

GREEN FINGERS

outdoor living

eat, sleep,
garden, repeat

TRANQUIL

outdoor space

hot tub

GYM crossfit

fitness

MARATHON

TONE UP

i am strong

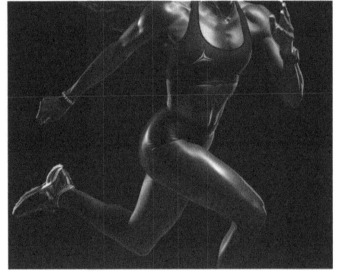

DOUBTING YOURSELF IS NORMAL. LETTING IT STOP YOU IS A CHOICE

HEALTHY

cardio

energised

BOOTCAMP

Beast Mode

ON!

stay
relentless

every rep
counts

DIG DEEP

beat your best

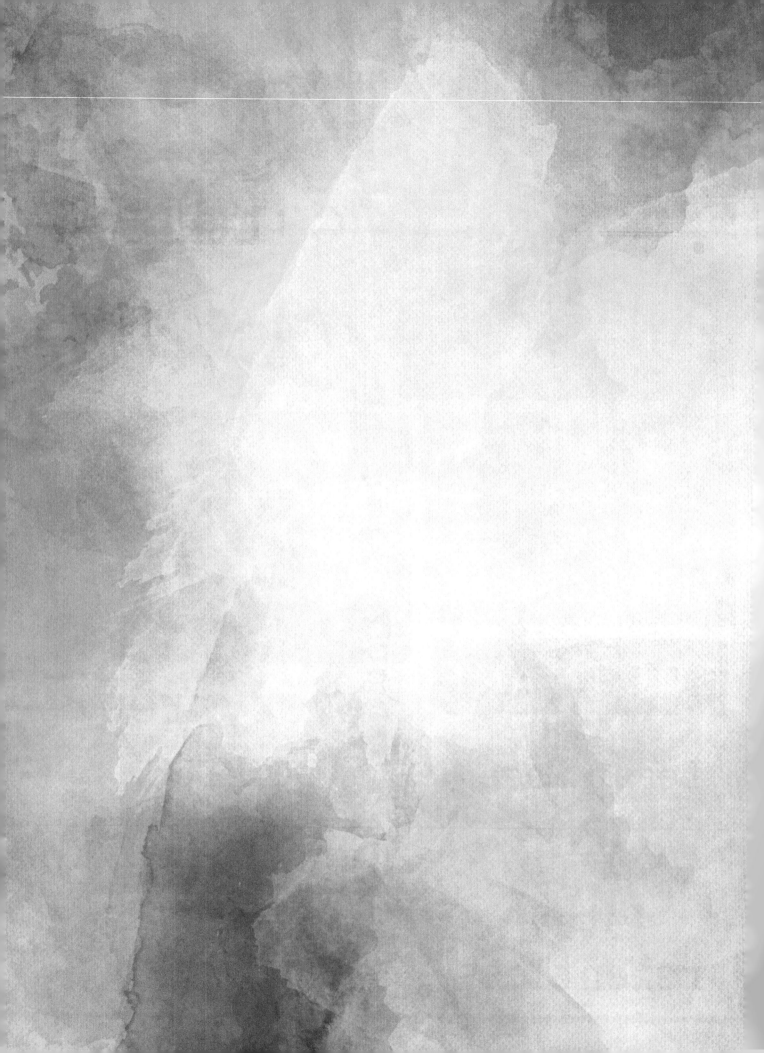

visualize your
highest self and
start showing up
as her

flexible

CONSISTENCY IS MORE IMPORTANT
THAN PERFECTION

nothing
changes if
nothing
changes

seek new heights

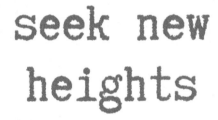

CONQUER

adventure

adventure is
the heartbeat
of the soul

ROCK CLIMBING

TRAIL RUNNING

fuel your passion

mastery

CHALLENGE

push

your

limits

surfing skiing

swimming

cycling

cardio

hiking

tennis

volleyball

weights

watersports

present moment

ME TIME

pamper

spa day

PAUSE

theta healing

SOUND BATH

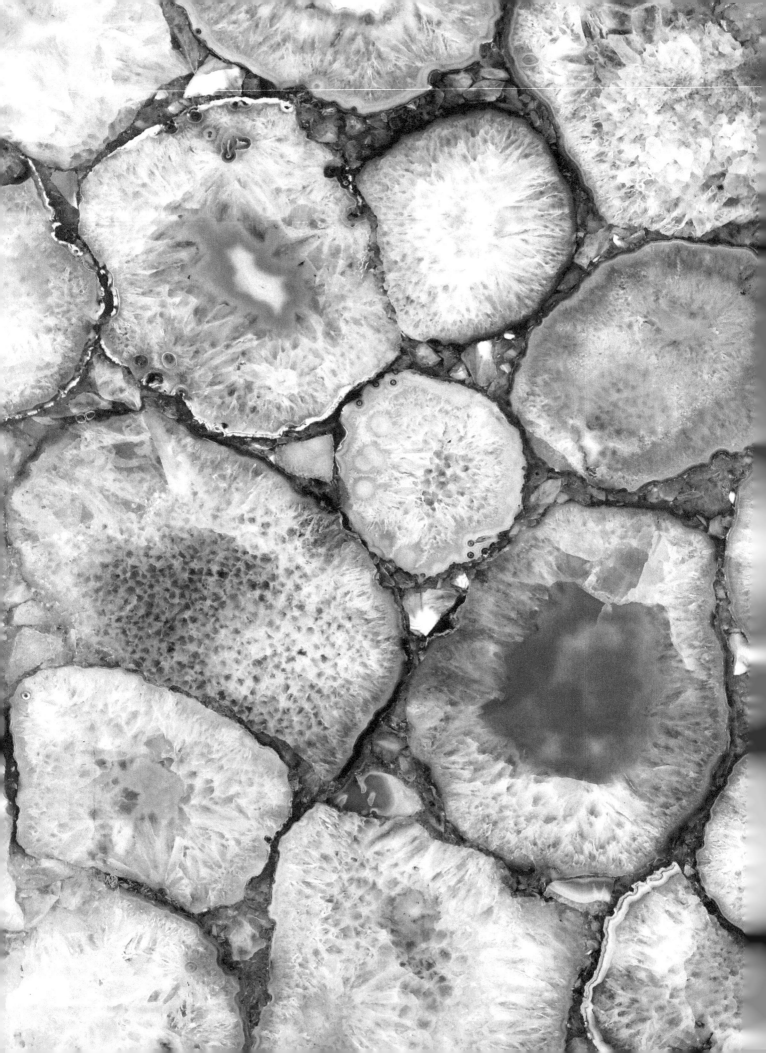

YOGA

retreat   choosing peace

follow your intuition

MEDITATE

I MAKE
TIME FOR
MYSELF

i love
my life

mindfulness

REJUVENATE

I choose to be kind to myself and love myself unconditionally

**I AM
WORTHY OF
BEAUTIFUL
FRIENDSHIPS**

**I AM RICH IN
ALL AREAS
OF MY LIFE**

**I AM
FINANCIALLY
FREE**

**I ATTRACT
POSITIVE
OPPORTUNITIES**

**I AM
RESILIENT**

**I LOVE MY
LUXURIOUS,
HEALTHY
LIFESTYLE**

**SOMETHING
WONDERFUL IS
ABOUT TO
HAPPEN TO ME**

**I AM LETTING
GO OF WHAT
I CAN'T
CONTROL**

**MY BODY IS
AMAZING**

**I ONLY
ATTRACT
HEALTHY
RELATIONSHIPS**

**I AM POWERFUL
ENOUGH TO
RESIST
TEMPTATIONS**

**I AM
SUCCESSFUL**

DIET

detox

nourish

REAL FOOD,
REAL BENEFITS

*I am
beautiful*

HEALTHY

LIVING

KETO

vegetarian

PLANT-BASED

hydrated

LOSE WEIGHT

eat to
thrive

ORGANIC

energise

VITALITY

food is
fuel, not
therapy

I AM HEALING MY
BODY WITH EACH
MOUTHFUL

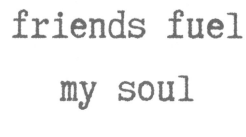
friends fuel
my soul

I ATTRACT
WONDERFUL
PEOPLE INTO
MY LIFE

SOUL SISTERS

BY MY
SIDE,
ALWAYS

third eye

I visualize, believe and receive

MANIFESTING IS
MY DIVINE RIGHT

TREASURE LOVE Breathe

magic SOUL Spiritual

FOCUSED

magical *I am strong* read

Heal SHARING INTUITION

RELAX CAREER My place

REST,

Weekend away self-care PEACE

RECHARGE THANKFUL Acceptance

Perspective FRIEND mighty

Eat well thrive FOREVER Soul

HEALTH Creative happier

FEELINGS I am enough SLEEP BETTER

DON'T STRESS Self-compassion TRUST

happiness

TRUE CALLING

RITUALS

Confidence

NEW DIRECTION

nurtured

visualise

pampering

move forward

transition

Meditation

Clarity

Hope

GOALS

WALK

POWERFUL

HEAL

HAPPY

self-compassion

CONFIDENT

positive

Learning

I am succeeding

I am loved

success

intimacy

New beginnings

ENERGY

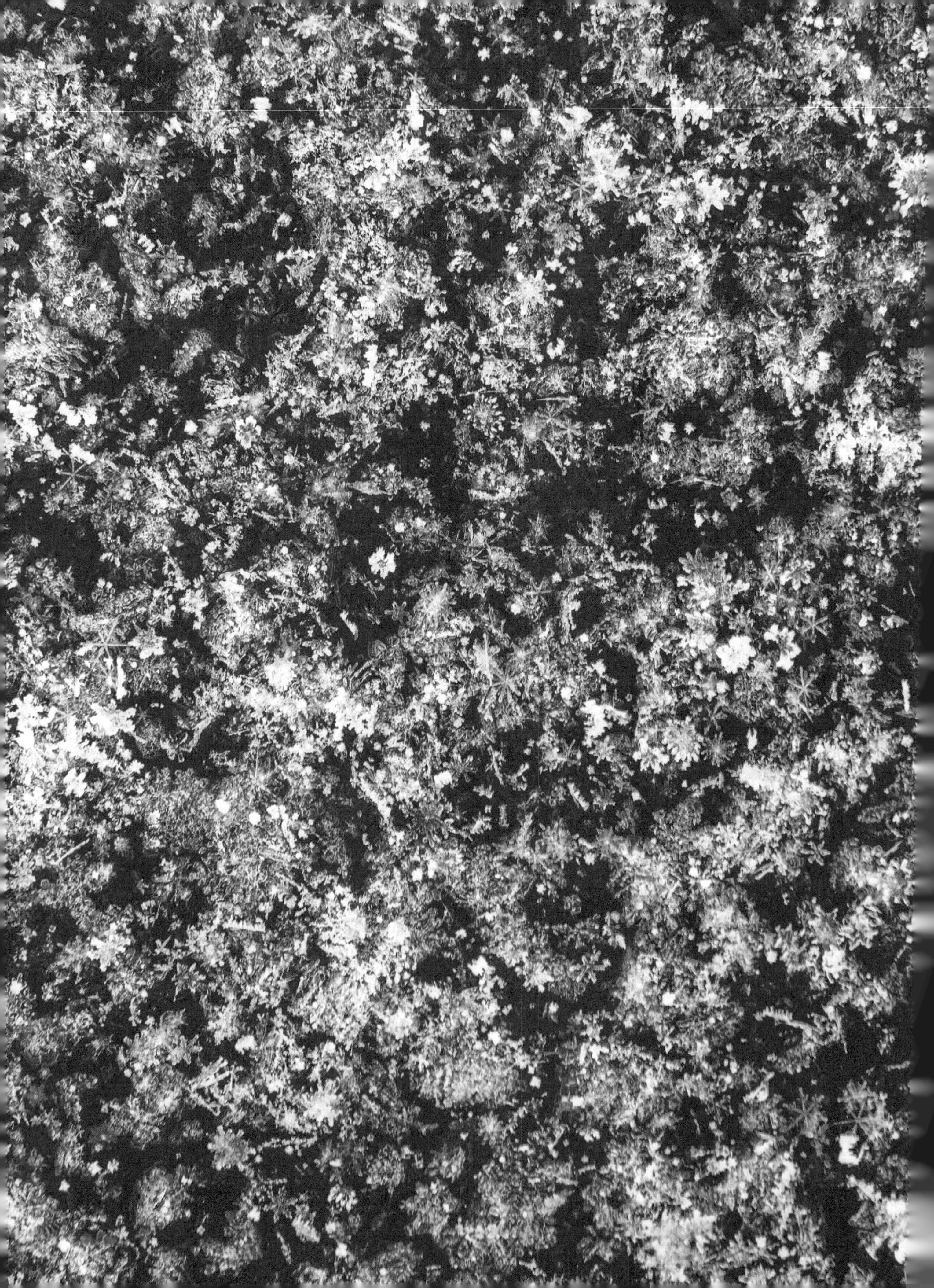

Positive energy *mindful*

Healthy **Retreat**

forgiveness *Love*

NATURE **self-confidence**

running CRUISING

DREAMS *travel*

POWERFUL CREATE

RECONNECT Gathering

INSPIRED Weekend away

happiness! HOME

thank♥you

We just wanted to take a moment to say thank you for choosing our vision board book We hope it's helping you manifest your dreams and inspiring you to be the best version of yourself.

We'd be over the moon if you could leave us a review on Amazon. We love reading your feedback - it gives us warm fuzzy feelings inside! And it helps us make our next books even better! ♥

Looking for even more images?

Subscribe to our newsletter and we'll send you a link to EVEN MORE downloadable images AND a FREE eBook that teaches you how to use the power of positive thinking and visualization to manifest your goals and desires. Scan the code below!

FREE E-BOOK

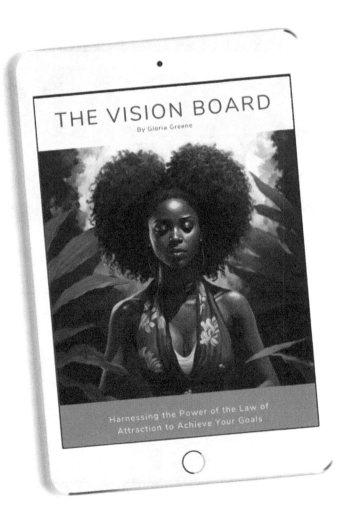

Scan this QR code to download your FREE downloadable images AND eBook.

Made in the USA
Las Vegas, NV
13 December 2023